T0361654

THE
WHITE LOTUS

ICONIC QUOTES
Heard Around the Resort

THE
WHITE LOTUS

ICONIC QUOTES
Heard Around the Resort

FROM THE HIT SERIES

INSIGHT ◆ EDITIONS

SAN RAFAEL · LOS ANGELES · LONDON

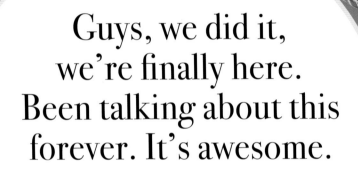

Guys, we did it, we're finally here. Been talking about this forever. It's awesome.

—Cameron

Contents

CHAPTER

1

Three's a Crowd

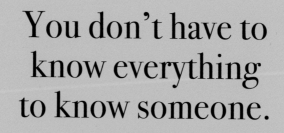

You don't have to know everything to know someone.

—Daphne

It's a wonderful thing
to make a . . . a new friend
so late in life.

—Didier

Don't spend your life
chasing emotionally
unavailable men. Or you'll
spend your whole life
just banging your head
against a wall.

— Tanya

You know, after hearing the story of your love life, we decided you were like a tragic heroine in a Puccini opera.

—Quentin

I don't wanna be a plus one my whole life.

—Rachel

Flirting is one of the pleasures of life.

—Bert

It's a warning to
husbands, babe.
Screw around and
you'll end up buried
in the garden.

—Daphne

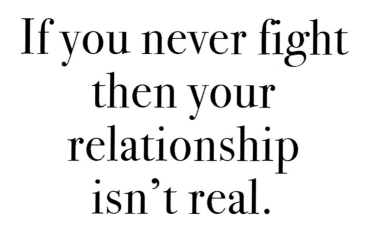

If you never fight then your relationship isn't real.

—Harper

I feel sorry for men,
you know. They think they're
out there doing something
really important, but really
they're just wandering alone.

—Daphne

Love's never been
my Achilles' heel.
It was always beauty.

—Quentin

I mean, we never really know
what goes on in people's minds
or what they do, right?
You spend every second
with somebody and there's still
this part that's a mystery.

—Daphne

Nobody loves you like your mother.

—Belinda

I just hope that we don't
become like one of those old,
depressing couples with all
this baggage and resentment
and regrets.

—Rachel

We are always gonna
feel like this.
We will always be young.
And we will always be in love.
And there will be days and
days just like this.

—Shane

Life's too short.
You know, we've got to
make the most out of
every moment . . .
but with each other.

—Mark

We have a connection.

—Pornchai

[S]he's my friend.
As long as she has more
of everything than I do.
But if I have something of
my own, she wants it.

—Paula

Listen.
I'm obsessed with you.
I wanna get you naked.
What do I gotta do?

—Armond

I just wanna meet someone who's like, you know, totally ignorant of the discourse.

—Portia

I mean, you know,
you don't want your kid
thinking you're some
sex-crazed lunatic.

—Mark

We're cosmically linked.

—Chelsea

I don't lie to my wife.

—Ethan

Dude, monogamy
was an idea created
by the elite to control
the middle class.

—Cameron

I put on
fresh underwear
for ya.

—Jack

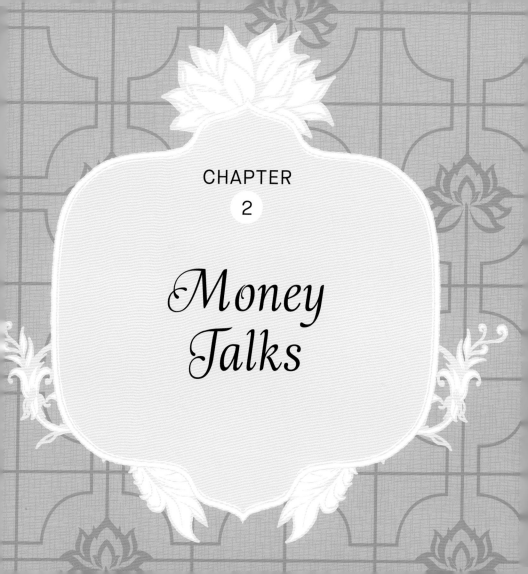

CHAPTER

2

Money Talks

Oh, it's a good feeling
when you realize someone
has money . . .
'Cause then you don't
have to worry about them
wanting yours.

—Tanya

I guess we're all snobs in different ways.

—Ethan

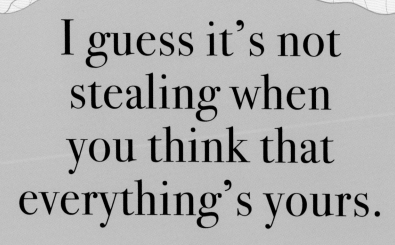

I guess it's not stealing when you think that everything's yours.

—Paula

Everybody's got to make their money somehow.

—Kitty

We have a stylist choose our outfits and then we have a book stylist pick out our books.

—Paula

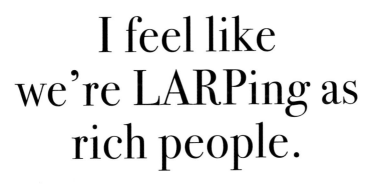

I feel like
we're LARPing as
rich people.

—Harper

Best thing about luck is,
it can always change.
—Quentin

Do you really believe that?
—Tanya

No.
—Quentin

The money, money, money.

—Kitty

Money, money, money.

—Shane

I love things.

— Chloe

If I had a half a billion dollars,
I would not be miserable.
I would be enjoying my life!

—Portia

They always say it's about the money, but it's not. It's not even about the room. They just need to feel seen. Seen. They wanna be the only child. The special, chosen baby child of the hotel. And we are their mean mummies, denying them their Pineapple room.

—Armond

You're too fabulous to be sad.

—Quentin

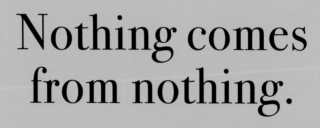

Nothing comes from nothing.

—Amrita

But I don't want to buy
the dress, Mia. I want to
buy the whole store.

—Lucia

Good things happen to good people.

—Nicole

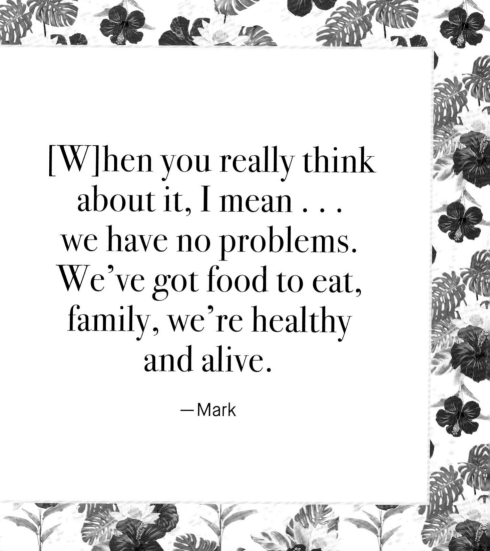

[W]hen you really think about it, I mean . . . we have no problems. We've got food to eat, family, we're healthy and alive.

—Mark

[I]f you have money, then that's what you bring to the table. You don't need to work.

—Kitty

I feel like if I won the lottery, I'd throw away the ticket.

—Portia

CHAPTER
3

Pride Comes Before the Fall

We're all just entertaining each other while the world burns, right?

—Harper

You know, I think . . . it's like
every kid . . . like, growing up,
wants to be the hero of the
story. And in the end . . .
you know, you're just happy
you're not the villain.

—Mark

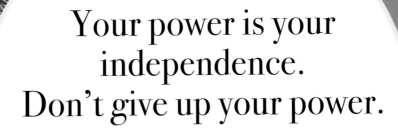

Your power is your independence.
Don't give up your power.

—Nicole

We're here on Earth
such a short time, but
our houses live on.
We must be good stewards.

—Quentin

You have a bad case of something called mimetic desire. If someone with higher status than you wants something, it means it's more likely that you'll want it, too.

—Ethan

The modern world today is just so . . . emasculating.

—Mark

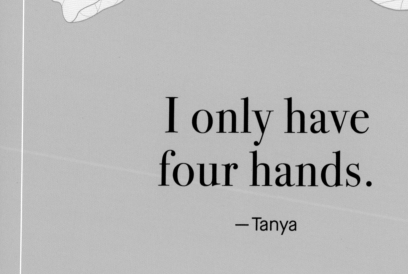

I only have four hands.

— Tanya

There's no virtuous person when we're all eating the last fish and throwing all our plastic crap in the ocean.

—Quinn

They just want
a better seat at the
table of tyranny.

—Nicole

I can't be responsible for everything I say.

—Bert

You know, when you're empty inside and you have no direction, you'll end up in some crazy places, right?
But you'll still be lost.

— Tanya

I'm a mystery to myself. Honestly, I surprise myself all the time.

—Daphne

Being a man, being a young man . . . in this time right now, can't be easy.

—Mark

Why? 'Cause we can't harass girls anymore?

—Quinn

No. Well, yeah.

—Mark

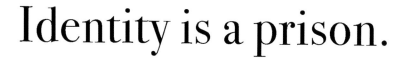

Identity is a prison.

—Por Teera

I do think that
there's a purpose
in helping
even rich people,
you know?

—Belinda

We're all just
trying to win
the game of life.

—Mark

CHAPTER
4

No Rest for the Wicked

They used to respect the old.
Now, we're just reminders
of an offensive past everybody
wants to forget.

—Bert

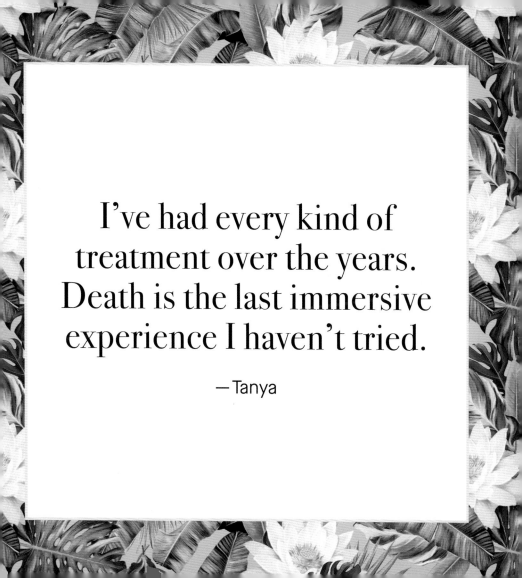

I've had every kind of treatment over the years. Death is the last immersive experience I haven't tried.

— Tanya

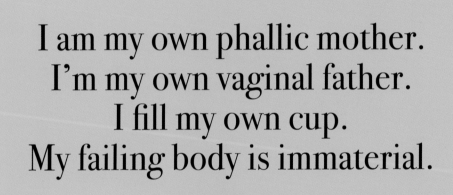

I am my own phallic mother.
I'm my own vaginal father.
I fill my own cup.
My failing body is immaterial.

—Belinda

It's healthy wine.

—Cameron

So, we can get drunk,
and then tomorrow
our skin, and our hair, and
our nails will be glowing.

—Daphne

Death doesn't have to
spoil everything, right?
Enjoy your life till they
drop the curtain.

—Greg

You're always being
born into life . . . like,
all the time.
You're not stuck . . .

—Mark

It's not healthy
to be so honest
all the time.

—Nicole

I don't do naps.

—Timothy

They're making breakthroughs every day. It's like a nonstop parade of progress.

—Nicole

I just feel like there must
have been a time
when the world had more.
You know? Like mystery
or something . . .

—Portia

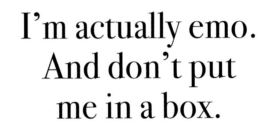

I'm actually emo.
And don't put
me in a box.

—Shane

Full-moon, baby!

—Saxon

We wanna be, like . . . superheroes and respectable fathers and pillars in our communities, whatever, but—but in fact, we're just monkeys . . . living in our own little monkey pods, driven by base instincts to create these hierarchies and hump each other.

—Mark

Dreams are a gateway.

—Piper

CHAPTER
5

Fortune Favors
the Bold

I really wanna get a job.

—Rachel

Honey, no. Why would
you want to do that?

—Kitty

Incompetence, it makes me homicidal.

—Cameron

All I do is everything I possibly can.

—Nicole

Making shit happen
all the time
is a compulsion.
It staves off feelings
of emptiness.
Or whatever.

—Olivia

I feel like if I murdered my boss, I could argue it was euthanasia.

—Portia

Most people admire
people who achieve things,
but you somehow look at it
as if it's a personality disorder.

—Nicole

It's because
you're nostalgic
for the solid days of
the patriarchy.

—Albie

I think you just . . .
you just . . . do whatever
you have to do not to
feel like a victim of life.

—Daphne

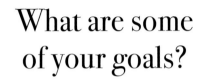

What are some of your goals?

—Jack

I don't know. Be satisfied? Yeah, that'd be nice.

—Portia

Her company is a part of the unraveling of the social fabric. Should I be rooting for that just because it's run by a woman?

—Olivia

No, you should be rooting for that because it's your mother.

—Nicole

My bad luck with assistants. They become my boss.

—Tanya

It's nice to know
you're really making
a difference
'cause sometimes,
I question that.

—Belinda

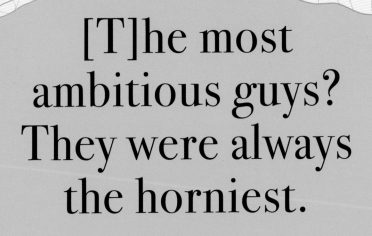

[T]he most ambitious guys? They were always the horniest.

—Cameron

Don't you think it's better
to just do what you want,
even if it's by yourself?

—Daphne

I just think it's funny
that I'm a role model
to strangers.

—Nicole

I was always gonna live life on my own terms. Obviously. But then what I manifested is . . . pretty mediocre.

—Rachel

Make sure it's not a cult.

—Victoria

Well, you're very magnetic,
and you're so beautiful.

—Kitty

You're making me sound
like a trophy wife.

—Rachel

Well, what's so wrong with that?
A trophy shines. It's a source of
pride. A trophy's made of gold.

—Kitty

CHAPTER
6

Time and Tide Wait for No One

You can't come to Sicily and just sit in your room. It's against the law.

—Bert

It's a breakfast buffet
in Hawaii!
It shouldn't be a
stressful situation!

—Quinn

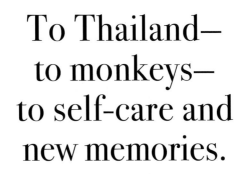

To Thailand—
to monkeys—
to self-care and
new memories.

—Laurie

You can't even get lost anymore 'cause you can just find yourself on Google Maps.

—Portia

Husbands murdering their wives. Happens a lot on vacation.

—Daphne

Well, I am a huge
advocate for distraction.
My whole life has been
one long distraction.

—Quentin

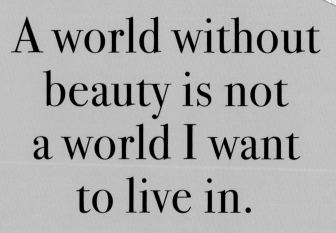

A world without beauty is not a world I want to live in.

—Quentin

You come somewhere like this
and it's beautiful and you
take a picture, and then you realize
that everybody's taken that
exact same picture from that exact
same spot. You just made
some redundant content, for
stupid Instagram.

—Portia

I am gonna give you what every girl in America wants, apparently. A trip to Burning Man in an electric RV that can levitate above the ground.

—Shane

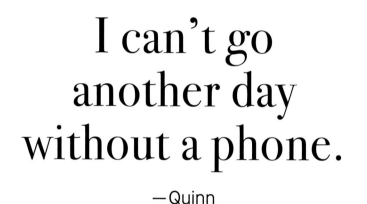

I can't go another day without a phone.

—Quinn

Mom, you
look deranged.

—Olivia

It's all right. I have
a filter for that.

—Nicole

We're living in the best time in
the history of the world—
on the best fucking planet.
If you can't be satisfied living
now, here, you're never
gonna be satisfied.

—Jack

The goal is to create for the guests an overall impression of vagueness that can be very satisfying, where they get everything they want but they don't even know what they want, or what day it is, or where they are, or who we are, or what the fuck is going on.

—Armond

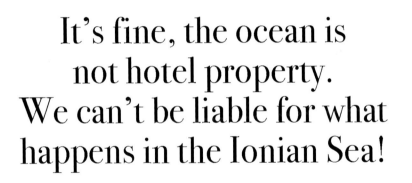

It's fine, the ocean is not hotel property. We can't be liable for what happens in the Ionian Sea!

—Valentina

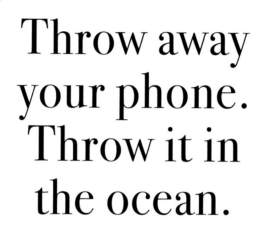

Throw away your phone. Throw it in the ocean.

—Albie

To volcanoes,
and all the threesomes
of the past and present
and future.

—Cameron

No one in the history of the world has lived better than we have. The least we can do is enjoy it! If we don't, it's offensive.

—Victoria

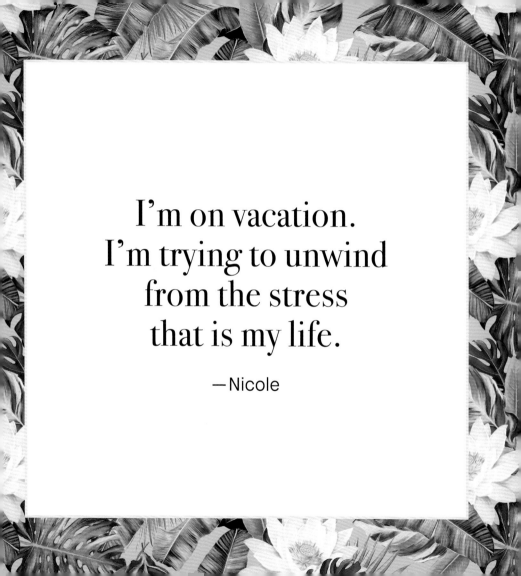

I'm on vacation.
I'm trying to unwind
from the stress
that is my life.

—Nicole

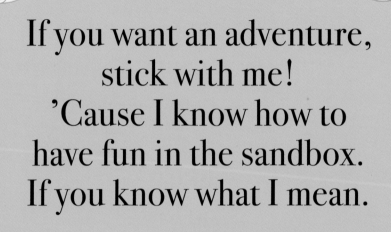

If you want an adventure,
stick with me!
'Cause I know how to
have fun in the sandbox.
If you know what I mean.

—Jack

It's our honeymoon.
I'm thinking a candlelit dinner
totally off on our own. Somewhere
cool that's like . . . a beach or a cliff
or just like . . . like an Instagram
spot, you know?

—Shane

PO Box 3088
San Rafael, CA 94912
www.insighteditions.com

Find us on Facebook: www.facebook.com/InsightEditions
Follow us on Instagram: @insighteditions

Copyright © 2025 Home Box Office, Inc.
THE WHITE LOTUS and all related characters and
elements © & ™ Home Box Office, Inc. (s25)

All rights reserved.

Published by Insight Editions,
San Rafael, California, in 2025.

No part of this book may be reproduced in any form
without written permission from the publisher.

ISBN: 979-8-88663-872-1

Publisher: Raoul Goff
SVP, Group Publisher: Vanessa Lopez
VP, Creative: Chrissy Kwasnik
VP, Manufacturing: Alix Nicholaeff
Editorial Director: Thom O'Hearn
Art Director: Stuart Smith
Senior Designer: Judy Wiatrek Trum
Editor: Alexis Sattler
Assistant Editor: Sami Alvarado
VP, Senior Executive Project Editor: Vicki Jaeger
Production Associate: Tiffani Patterson
Senior Production Manager, Subsidiary Rights:
Lina s Palma-Temena

Manufactured in China by Insight Editions

10 9 8 7 6 5 4 3 2 1

 REPLANTED PAPER

Insight Editions, in association with Roots of
Peace, will plant two trees for each tree used in the
manufacturing of this book. Roots of Peace is an
internationally renowned humanitarian organization
dedicated to eradicating land mines worldwide and
converting war-torn lands into productive farms
and wildlife habitats. Roots of Peace will plant two
million fruit and nut trees in Afghanistan and provide
farmers there with the skills and support necessary for
sustainable land use.